Rescued By A Cow and A Squeeze
~ Temple Grandin ~

by
Mary Carpenter

PUBLISH AMERICA

PublishAmerica
Baltimore

First printing

Author's Note: At the request of Temple Grandin, some
names of people and places have been changed.

ISBN: 1-59129-880-6
PUBLISHED BY PUBLISHAMERICA BOOK
PUBLISHERS
www.publishamerica.com
Baltimore

Printed in the United States of America

For my family – Oliver who was intrigued by Temple's story; Edmund who kept my nose to the grindstone; and Adam who edited the final drafts. And for Dr. Oliver Sacks who encouraged me to write Temple's story for children.

ACKNOWLEDGEMENTS

I would like to thank Sally Smith who, through lectures, books and The Lab School of Washington, taught me about children with learning disabilities. She showed me how much these children are inspired by successful people with similar disabilities.

Of course, I offer immeasurable thanks to Temple Grandin who helped me so much and so frequently, with patience and directness, and with an incredibly honest and thorough understanding of herself – of the person she became and of how she got there.

Finally I thank my friends – Susie Allport for planting the seed of this book – and all the others, including my writing group, who provided non-stop encouragement and editing help: Natalie Wexler, Ellen Cassedy, Sally Steenland, Jenny Brody, Sara Taber, Anne Glusker and Cathy Trost; and Janet Bennett, Susan Spock, Susan Land, Paulette Perrien and Polly Kracora. And I thank PublishAmerica for supporting first-time authors and working hard to make books like this possible.

PROLOGUE

Beef cows are raised for their meat. The beef cow's huge mass of fat and muscle can weigh as much as a small elephant – up to one ton, which is 2,000 pounds. Unlike dairy cows, their slender sisters which produce milk, beef cows grow quickly. Beef cows spend their days grazing in fields and then move to the large pens of industrial feedlots where they eat and eat and eat.

What are these beef cows thinking as they chew their endless dinners? How do they react to the sights and sounds around them? What makes them happy or scared as they move in long, snaking lines onto trucks and into new corrals?

When a girl named Temple Grandin saw her first beef cow, she knew immediately how to answer these questions. Temple believed right away that beef cows heard and saw just like she did. Therefore, she thought, their experience of the world must be the same as hers.

Temple watched cows become upset by unpredictable noises and unexpected objects in their wide fields of vision. She reacted the same way. Temple observed their agitation when they slid and lost their balance on the slanted metal ramps beneath their hooves. She noticed that cows appear happiest when walking in a circular chute or following another cow; when they believe they know where they're going. And once cows become upset, she saw that they remain upset for hours before being able to calm down. All these responses were just like hers.

Most important for her own life, Temple saw how relaxed a cow becomes in a "squeeze chute," where the walls of a narrow corridor move inward to hold a cow still for branding, vaccinations and other veterinary treatments. As the sides of the chute tightened, she saw the cow's eyes grow calm.

Only after she observed cows did this young woman begin to move quickly into a brilliant career. Temple Grandin became a professor of animal science and a designer of architectural innovations that improved the lives of cows and other livestock.

***

But as a child, Temple Grandin struggled with overwhelming disabilities both in learning and in getting along with other people. She was at the bottom of her class in every subject, and was expelled from the local junior high school because of her aggressive behavior with classmates and teachers. Eventually, with the help of cows, Temple found that she had amazing strengths, such as the ability to concentrate intensely and to create detailed architectural designs entirely in her mind.

Brilliant people sometimes have trouble with language or math or getting along with others. "Be proud you are different," Mrs. Grandin urged her discouraged daughter. "All bright people who have contributed to life have been different and found the path of life lonely. While the joiners and social butterflies flutter about, Temple, you'll get real things done."

Mrs. Grandin was right. Many creative people – from Albert Einstein, the physicist; to Vincent Van Gogh, the artist; to Bill Gates, the computer software inventor – had trouble either doing well in school or dealing with people. But they accomplished great deeds. Not only did Temple Grandin become a well-known inventor who improved the lives of animals, but she gave lectures around the country and wrote two autobiographical books that offered the world a rare glimpse inside her different kind of mind.

Temple at age 2 1/2

CHAPTER ONE: TEMPLE'S BRAIN

Temple's Beginnings

On June 4, 1947, the first of Jim and Julia Grandin's four children was born. They named her Temple, an old family surname from England. Surrounding the Grandin house, on its pleasant street of old mansions in a wealthy Boston suburb, was a large, tree-filled yard. Neighbors couldn't hear the screaming tantrums of baby Temple, which could last all morning or late into the night.

At age two and a half, Temple had charming blue eyes, a mass of downy brown hair and a dimple in her chin. But while most children at that age are using many words and often speak in whole sentences, Temple didn't talk and didn't respond to speech. Boston's best doctors pronounced her deaf. In the 1950s, children who couldn't talk were considered retarded, and those with unruly behavior like Temple's were often sent away to live in hospital-like institutions. But Temple's mother worked hard to help her little girl at home.

In fact, Temple could hear. But individual sounds, especially consonants, blurred together with other noises around her so that she couldn't distinguish words. If someone said, "Eat your peas," Temple heard a static-filled mish-mash that sounded something like "Eeyore" with a faint "pee" at the end. Unable to hear properly, she couldn't learn the words to ask for what she wanted, and so she rocked and screamed in frustration.

When she turned five, doctors determined that Temple had a condition of the brain called autism.

The senses of autistic children are so finely tuned that the morning sunshine can feel as blinding as a flashlight shined in the eyes. Dinner can smell like a barnyard. And human conversation can sound like an onrushing freight train. Autistic children react with furious tantrums or withdraw entirely from this world they find overwhelming.

***

One day when she was six and dressed in a sweet, blue gingham frock, Temple lay on the floor of a Boston clothes store kicking and clawing as other shoppers looked on in horror. Temple's young mother scooped up her daughter and tried to calm her with a hug, but Temple kicked out again with her strong legs and fell back onto the floor. Spewing out garbled sounds, she began to rock and howl. What she couldn't say was that the store was too bright and the people too noisy, and that her mother's hugs made her afraid she might suffocate to death.

But Mrs. Grandin knew Temple needed to get out of the store. The minute they arrived home, she took her distraught daughter upstairs to her room where Temple liked to squeeze into a small space between her single bed and the wall. There she sat on the pale blue floor boards and rocked and rocked until the outside world faded away. The quiet darkness of her mind enveloped her. She made meaningless noises and told stories aloud to create a separate, inner peace. Soon she felt better.

***

A Mother's Help

Mrs. Grandin understood how to help her daughter even though doctors at the time knew very little about autism. In fact, they blamed the parents, especially the mother, saying that their cold and distant behavior forced the child to withdraw from the world. Experts believed autistic children were not intelligent, could not attend regular school and would not be able to support themselves as independent adults.

After doctors said Temple was deaf, her mother enrolled her in a speech therapy program, where teachers stretched out the way they pronounced consonants, like the "t" in "eatttt," until Temple could begin to pick out sounds and understand words. Soon she could talk – though her words had an unusual sound and could be hard to understand, especially when she was upset. And Temple still felt too overwhelmed to look people in the eye. "Temple, are you listening to me?" her mother would ask over and over.

Mrs. Grandin set aside a special time each day after lunch when Temple could rock in her room. Temple's autism also made her a pressure seeker, but she needed to find pressure that she could control. In the afternoons, she liked to wrap herself in blankets and bury herself under the sofa cushions because she found the pressure against her body so relaxing. Babies for centuries have been swaddled tightly for comfort, and many kids like special places where they can escape to be alone. But Temple's autism made her needs for pressure and escape more desperate and last long beyond childhood.

Pressure she couldn't control, like tight hugs and clothes, sent Temple into a panic. As a small child in the car with her mother and younger sister, Jean, she almost caused a terrible accident. The hat she was wearing, which her mother said looked so nice, made Temple's ears feel squashed. But when she took it off, the hat waited on her lap like a hot and prickly monster. Suddenly Temple threw the hat out the window, and her mother, reaching to catch it, swerved into the path of a tractor-trailer. The car window shattered, and Temple screamed, "Ice, ice, ice," at the cascading glass fragments, one of her first clearly-spoken words.

Family Life

The Grandin family's formal and structured life helped keep Temple's autistic symptoms under control. The four children – Temple, her sister Jean who was a year younger, and another sister and a brother, both almost ten years younger – dressed up for Sunday dinner. They were corrected constantly for bad manners or poor grammar, such as when Temple said, "Jean and me want ice cream" instead of "Jean and I."

Miss Cray, a strict nanny with gray hair pulled into a tight bun, was hired to organize the lives of Temple and Jean. Miss Cray played games with them and filled their free hours with activities like sledding and skating. Miss Cray understood Temple's extreme sensitivities, especially to noise, but she also knew how to help Temple stay focused. One night at the dinner table when her charge became distracted and misbehaved, Miss Cray said, "If you don't finish your soup right now, I'll pop a bag at you." She blew up a brown sandwich bag and burst it in Temple's face. Whereas for most children this treatment would be cruel, Temple understood that it worked well to get her attention back to the food.

When Temple chewed up a jigsaw puzzle or had a screaming tantrum, her mother cancelled that day's *Howdy Doody* TV show. But she could tell when Temple required extra help, such as patiently-explained examples of what was right and wrong. Once Temple stole a new toy fire engine from a little boy's birthday party. Because she had so much trouble understanding how people get along, it took hours to convince her she would not like someone to steal one of her model airplanes and to return the fire engine.

CHAPTER TWO: EARLY SCHOOL DAYS

Temple's Strengths

During most of her childhood and teenage years, Temple felt afraid – like a wary animal. Because she had such difficulty feeling comfortable with the sights and sounds around her, small changes such as new red curtains on the kitchen window made her whole world seem scary. Big changes like a new school were terrifying.

After kindergarten, Temple moved to Valley Country Day, a private elementary school outside Boston. Luckily, there were small classes of only twelve children – instead of the twenty or thirty students common in most schools – and, like Temple's family, class was run in an old-fashioned, orderly way, with each child taking his or her turn.

Temple's disability gave her amazing strengths – like observation, concentration and logic. By blocking out overwhelming sights and sounds, she could concentrate intensely, sitting for hours on the beach dribbling sand through her fingers. Each particle of sand – its color, size and shape – intrigued her as though she were a scientist.

An extraordinary ability to create pictures in her mind made Temple adept at problem solving and gave her an excellent visual memory. When she found the Lord's Prayer impossible to understand, much less memorize, she fixed her attention on the prayer for hours. She figured out how to transform the phrases into mental images. To understand "the power and the glory," she pictured an electrical tower with lights for the power and a brightly-colored rainbow for the glory. "Thy will be done" became a God-like figure throwing a lightning bolt. Once the prayer made sense, remembering it was easy.

To solve problems, Temple immersed herself in daydreams as vivid to her as feature-length movies. She would make a detailed picture in her head and then make that picture come alive and move like a video inside her head – again and again, over hours or weeks or years – until she found a solution. Temple's memory worked like a video library where she could file away all the moving pictures she'd ever made in case she needed them again.

Temple's Progress

By third grade, Temple became able to hear more clearly and to separate words from background noises, which slowly became less bothersome. But when she still hadn't learned to read, her mother set aside one hour each day to teach Temple phonics, a method of sounding out parts of a word until the whole word becomes clear. At tea time, the two would sit at an old farmhouse table in the sunny kitchen, a moment of calm together before dinner preparations began. Her enthusiasm for the grown-up tea ceremony – in fact, she drank hot water with lemon juice and just a hint of tea flavoring – made Temple want learn. By the end of the year, she enjoyed reading, especially biographies. Her favorite was about Clara Barton, founder of the American Red Cross.

***

Temple's mother kept a diary. One day she wrote, "When she's bored or tired, Temple spits or takes off her shoes and throws them...I must say though that even on her worst days, she is intelligent and exciting."

***

Temple's grandfather, her mother's father, lived alone in a nearby Boston suburb. Sometimes her mother brought Temple to visit Grandfather Barstow, a tall, burly man with twinkling eyes who had the time, patience and knowledge to answer his granddaughter's many questions. "What makes the tides go in and out?" Temple would ask. Her grandfather, who invented an automatic pilot system for airplanes, could explain in scientific detail about the effects of the moon rotating around the earth. Not only did Temple learn from him, but she also probably inherited his engineering ability.

Temple's parents separated when she was about ten, after which she rarely saw her father. But she had clear memories of him, especially of days spent on his motor boat. "You are the best polisher in the world," he told her after a day of boat cleaning. They both liked physical activity. Although her father was a businessman, not an engineer, he and Temple enjoyed making things and figuring out how things worked. Temple's father bought her math blocks to explain how numbers relate to each other, and a book on perspective drawing to show how to create three-dimensional images on flat surfaces.

Squeezes

By fourth grade, Temple began to dream of a magical device that would provide intense, pleasant pressure that she could control. Like many children with learning disabilities, she continued to shrink from the wrong kind of touch. Her Aunt Ida endeared herself to Temple by sharing her professional oil paints, but she gave hugs that made Temple feel like she was being suffocated by a mountain of marshmallows.

Temple's first idea was an inflatable suit that squeezed

the body. By the end of elementary school, she had moved on to imagining a long box with moving sides that gave both pressure and warmth. These ideas stayed with her for many years.

Obsessions and Friends

At ten years old, Temple could be very annoying. She asked non-stop questions, laughed uncontrollably and became so completely absorbed in her own thoughts she couldn't be budged. Some of her interests became extreme obsessions– such as politics, especially the election of her state governor. She talked constantly about campaign posters, buttons, bumper stickers and flags. With Eleanor Griffin, who had been Temple's best friend throughout elementary school, she stole huge election posters from telephone poles and tacked them up in her room. The same extreme concentration that led to Temple's obsessions, however, later gave her the single-mindedness to concentrate on goals until she succeeded.

Temple made up stories about an imaginary cast of characters and, no matter where she happened to be, told the stories out loud. As the bad guy, she cast a classmate named Alfred Costello, who tormented her with names like "dummie" and "weirdo." In Temple's stories, Alfred got into trouble with authorities like the police. Whenever teachers caught him misbehaving in school, Temple would laugh loudly for a long time, even during class.

Despite her difficult behavior, Temple's original ideas helped her make good friends at Valley Country Day. When the school had a pet show, Temple got a lot of laughs because she brought herself, dressed as a dog, with two friends who were twins as her masters. For the whole day she performed like a dog – barking, sitting up, lying down – and was such a big hit she received a blue ribbon. The next year at the class toy show, Temple went as a rag doll. At home or with these friends, her odd mannerisms calmed down. Temple had no idea how different she seemed.

***

One day when Temple was spinning around on the swings and giggling with Eleanor and another friend, Crystal Swift, Alfred Costello walked up and screamed at Temple, "Chatterbox! Crystal, why do you play with that chatterbox?"

"Because she's not boring," yelled Crystal, going into a fast spin. "I like Temple."

"I do, too," chimed in Eleanor, who was pushing off on a nearby swing. "Temple makes neat things that you couldn't dream of, Alfred Costello."

With three girls against him, Alfred slunk quietly away.

***

Art classes were Temple's favorite because she loved to draw and build. She fascinated her classmates by designing lively puppets and an intricate toy gas station. Creating her own paper kite to fly behind her tricycle, Temple found that if she bent a little flap on the ends of each wing, the kite would fly at a steeper angle. Years later, Temple saw a corporate jet with the same little flaps on the ends of the wings and recognized what she had invented long ago.

***

For show-and-tell, classmates crowded around to watch Temple launch the model helicopter she'd designed. On the first try, when the kids didn't expect much to happen, Temple's model flew almost 100 feet straight up, higher than the playground's tallest tree.

"See what Temple can make," Eleanor called out. Eleanor often had to stick up for her buddy, because Temple could barely understand the class work, had screaming and biting tantrums in the school hall and smacked her classmates. But not today. All the kids had questions for Temple about her helicopter. What made it fly so high? How did she attach the propeller?

***

Temple's sensitivity to noise ruined special events like birthday parties or a ride on the ferryboat with its loud horn on the way to the family's summer house. School, where she was constantly bombarded by kids pushing against her and the noises of bells and whistles, made her feel like she was inside a pinball machine.

Temple's report cards showed Ds and Fs. Because she didn't understand the teachers most of the time, she became bored, and boredom made her naughty. She tied the cords of window shades to the students' desks so that, when they opened the desks, the shades fell down. Temple was a bad sport at games and had a terrible temper. One day she got so mad that she threw herself on the floor and kicked everyone who came near. Another day, she bit a teacher's leg until it bled.

She told her math teachers she saw no point in doing multiplication. And one day during French class, Temple told her teacher to "*Ferme la bouche*," or shut your mouth.

"How can you be so rude and belligerent in French class yet so well behaved in sewing?" asked the teacher, who also taught sewing.

"Simple," answered Temple. "In sewing class, I can create something." In fifth grade, Temple helped make most of the costumes for the school play.

CHAPTER THREE: COWS AND
THE SQUEEZE MACHINE

Changing Schools

At the end of sixth grade, Temple entered junior high at Cherry Hill Girls' School outside Boston, where she had much more freedom and much more anxiety. It was the worst period of her life. For the first time, Temple's classes were large, with thirty or more kids. Every day brought new panic attacks. She compared herself to a windmill in a tornado, or a tiger pacing in a cage or an actor with stage fright that never went away. Fear, caused by loud noises and bright lights as well as any change in her routine, made Temple's heart pound, her palms sweat and her legs twitch. Temple began to be afraid of fear itself, that she might have a panic attack without warning and lose control in a crowd of strangers.

While these fears created havoc inside Temple's brain and stomach, the Cherry Hill students teased her mercilessly. Crossing the school parking lot, Temple heard classmates call out names like "Stoo-pid" and "Ree-tard" until she wanted to disappear. These insults upset Temple more than Alfred Costello's badgering. Because friends like Eleanor and Crystal had gone to other schools, she felt alone with her fears.

But Temple's own behavior was unpleasant as well. She didn't hesitate to tell other students that their projects were "simple" or "dumb ideas." One classmate told her, "Some of your remarks would alienate a viper." After two years of junior high, Temple's tantrums, during which she hit other students and almost blinded one girl, got her expelled from Cherry Hill.

Then her mother discovered a boarding school in the Vermont countryside with only 32 students and very small classes. After a long drive through snowy mountains, Temple saw cottage-sized school buildings and a large barn nestled among the pine and maple trees, and immediately felt encouraged. The school owned horses and other farm animals, and a dairy where students could work.

Mr. Carlock

At Mountain Country School, Temple found the first of a series of creative, unconventional people who believed in her. Mr. Carlock, the science teacher, rescued Temple from classmates as he guided her through the difficulties of his subject. Mr. Carlock liked kids who were intelligent and good at making things, and he recognized both of these qualities in Temple. He also ran the model rocket club where Temple made lots of rockets, including one that looked like the school principal.

Looking back, Temple believed that Mr. Carlock was what's called a "visual thinker" – like her. Temple used to say, "Pictures are my first language; English is my second." Mr. Carlock understood that Temple learned best with lots of photographs and charts, and he made puppets to demonstrate scientific principles.

While many students and other teachers became unnerved by Temple's endless questions, Mr. Carlock gave her books by philosophers. He encouraged her to talk with him about age-old questions, such as "Does God exist?"

At Mountain Country School, Temple helped build a house and shingle a barn. In most other schools at the time, these activities were offered only to boys. She also discovered horses, and for the first time felt a special understanding for animals, much more than she had for the dogs and cats of her childhood. Temple quickly became an accomplished rider. When a horse behaved badly, Temple didn't think the solution was harsh discipline. Instead, she believed that – like her – the horse was upset or afraid.

Learning about Cows

During this time, Temple's mother remarried, and along with a new step-father, Temple gained an aunt who owned a ranch in Arizona. At the end of eleventh grade, Temple visited Aunt Anne's ranch and stayed for six weeks. She liked being a cowboy and wearing jeans, flannel shirts and boots. And she loved being with her aunt's cows, muscular breeds raised for beef. Temple could hardly believe she'd found a place on earth where she truly belonged.

For hours each day, Temple watched and touched the cows and, beneath her hands, felt them grow calm. When the time came for young calves to get branded or vaccinated, Temple ran with them through the narrow chutes, corridors lined with fences on both sides which are used to move cows from one place to another. She watched the chutes narrow to a place where each cow's head is positioned in a head gate, and the wooden walls of the chute move inward against the cow's ribs to hold it tight. As walls closed in on the cow's body, Temple saw the cow become very calm.

Eventually Temple knew cows so well, she could picture herself inside the body of a 1200 pounder. She felt what it would be like to push up against other cattle and to navigate the chutes. As Temple was learning about cows, the cows taught her important lessons about herself – about what to avoid and how to relax. She got new ideas for the squeeze machine she'd dreamed about in fourth grade.

Most people considered Temple's behavior odd, but she had discovered a passion. Temple's ability to see the world "through a cow's eye" saved her life and led her into an exciting career.

Temple gets a cow's view of the world.
©Photo by Rosalie Winard

The Squeeze Chute

"I want to make a cattle chute for people like me," Temple Grandin told Mr. Carlock when she got back from the ranch.

"For people? A cattle chute?" Mr. Carlock was alarmed.

"Yes. I think cows are a lot like me. One day I got into the cattle chute at my aunt's ranch," said Temple.

"Wait. You got inside a squeeze chute?" asked Mr. Carlock, horrified and, at the same time, intrigued. "What happened?"

"She tightened it, and I felt good."

Now fascinated, Mr. Carlock asked, "What was the feeling exactly?"

"Calm," Temple explained. "I became calm. Just like the cows. And I stayed calm for almost an hour."

She asked Mr. Carlock how to find someone to build a machine that squeezed people. He told her, "We start with you, Temple."

***

As Mr. Carlock wrote in an introduction to one of Temple's autobiographies, "I found myself being pulled into her fascinating world of cattle chutes and becalmed calves. I know I've seen the human spirit at its best."

***

Now Temple had a goal, and someone who believed in that goal. Before her summer on the cattle ranch, Temple's disabilities prevented her from doing well at school. But Mr. Carlock convinced her she needed to learn math and science to understand more about the relaxing effects of pressure. With the goal of building a squeeze machine,

Temple was so motivated to study that she could block out social difficulties and other distractions. Her fearfulness diminished, and her bright and focused brain mastered these subjects. No longer an academic failure, Temple completed high school with good enough grades to go on to college.

Every weekend, Mr. Carlock took Temple to work on the squeeze machine in his laboratory, which became her refuge from a world she didn't understand. Almost everyone else, even Temple's mother, thought a box that squeezed people was weird and unhealthy, and they pushed Temple to give it up and be "more normal." Instead, their criticisms drove Temple even harder to prove she could make something important and useful, and her persistence paid off.

Before the end of high school, Temple built a prototype of the squeeze machine. Its foam-padded panels could be moved gently inward using a joystick to squeeze the person inside. When Temple climbed into the machine and tightened the panels, the soothing pressure helped her relax. Afterwards, she could endure brief physical contact from others: shaking hands became less unpleasant. After more improvements, a manufacturing company agreed to produce the "Big Squeeze," and clinics around the country used it to calm children with autism and hyperactivity.

Temple earned no royalties from production of the Big Squeeze or from its use by others. She said, "I didn't make as much money as I could have, because my main motivation was to make improvements. I consider my life a success if I can create change for the better." Temple made enough money to support herself comfortably – which is highly unusual for someone diagnosed with autism – from her businesses and from one invention for which she obtained a patent. Wherever she lived, Temple kept the squeeze machine she'd built especially for herself.

CHAPTER FOUR: TEMPLE'S DESTINY

After High School

Temple was admitted to Franklin Pierce College in New Hampshire, not far from Mountain Country School and Mr. Carlock. He continued to work with her on the squeeze machine and, as she said, kept her from "falling apart" in the turmoil of college. Another teacher, the art professor at college, taught Temple a crucial lesson when she assigned the class to spend two entire hours sketching an old tennis shoe. The drawing Temple produced of the shoe showed her how much more she could achieve with her talents at observation and art when she worked slowly.

Not only did Temple finish college, but she continued her education at graduate school in Animal Science, attending part time at Arizona State University and later at the University of Illinois. For the first time, she went out into the world on her own, thousands of miles away from both her family and Mr. Carlock. Temple earned a Ph.D., the highest degree possible in education.

She wanted to write her graduate thesis on the behavior

of cattle in different types of chutes – those made of different materials such as metal or concrete, or different shapes such as straight chutes or curved ones. But because research on farm livestock – including cattle, sheep, pigs and many other animals – was rare in the early 1970s, her professors refused to accept the project.

Again Temple persevered until she found support elsewhere. Her research demonstrated that some chute designs were more likely than others to injure animals. Once the cows or sheep were in the squeeze part of the chute, Temple also determined the exact number of minutes and seconds that should be allowed for vaccinations and other procedures so that the animals wouldn't get hurt.

While attending part-time graduate school, Temple began her career handling cows for the country's largest meat producers. By the time she started her own company, she had been employed by every brand name represented in the meat section of a large supermarket including Excel, Con Agra and IBP Tyson.

With her graduate degrees, Temple succeeded in finding a rare teaching job as Associate Professor of Animal Science at Colorado State University. She moved to an apartment in Fort Collins with the vast Rocky Mountains outside her window, where she continued to live for most of her adult life.

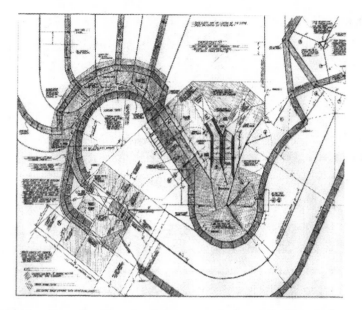

Blueprint drawn by Temple shows curved chutes for livestock.

The Chutes Lead to a New Career

Temple began to make improvements on chute designs that would reduce stress on cows. She made drawings of her improvements. Slowly she developed a reputation and then a career that combined her artistic and design abilities with her intimate knowledge of cows.

By this time, too, Temple had discovered something important about herself. If she wanted to learn something new, she needed to do it her own way. In order to improve cattle building designs, she had to learn how to read and draw blueprints, the original, highly detailed designs from which buildings are constructed. But she did not go back to school.

To teach herself how to read blueprints, one day she walked through an entire cattle plant with a blueprint of the plant in her hand. When she located the actual wall or surface represented by each line in the drawing, she felt like a magician making a picture become real. Temple found holding tanks represented by circles, square shop columns by squares, and large vats by ovals.

To learn how to draw a blueprint – called drafting – she intently watched a co-worker, whom she called "Davey the draftsman," day after day as he made thousands of tiny lines, each measured perfectly, for complex architectural designs.

Using a ruler to measure each line forced Temple to slow down even more. And when she slowed down, she stumbled onto a new talent that made all the difference. It turned out that Temple could trace complicated designs in her mind. Then, she could make that mental blueprint into a moving picture inside her head, like a video. While she was drawing, she could imagine how each part would function. When she'd finished, Temple could check the operation of her design in real life by watching her moving mental model from any point of view – that of a cow running through her building or of a helicopter observing from above.

To put together the new skills of reading and drafting blueprints, again Temple worked on her own. She walked around a large feedlot filled with pens that hold tens of thousands of cattle at one time, and measured each surface. Then she returned to her desk and created exact replicas of the original blueprints, including each of the thousands of lines.

Self-training made Temple a draftsman – able to create original designs for her inventions. The engineer on a project normally comes in to work after the draftsman has finished. But Temple could do a lot of the engineering work on a project as well, despite her serious difficulties with math. She said, "I'm an engineer because of my ability to visualize."

Temple might not have discovered her remarkable ability – to visualize a detailed design and make it come alive in her mind as she was drawing it for the first time – if she had never encountered cows and recognized her special understanding of them. Or if she hadn't had a Mr. Carlock who believed in her.

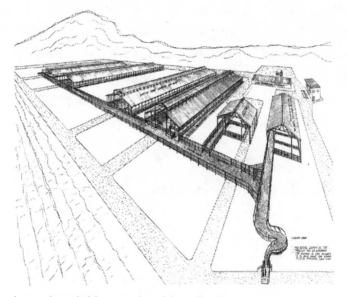

Temple produced this complete blueprint in one try.

Her Work Becomes a Success

In Temple's new world of ranches and cattle, men had always done the work. Temple wondered whether the biggest obstacle to her success was being autistic or being a woman. Both qualities got in her way, but both may also have given her an increased sensitivity to the animals and to the deeper questions raised about livestock destined to be killed for food.

Some people stop eating meat because they worry about animal suffering – but many, like Temple, who continue to eat meat, are equally concerned about animal welfare. Temple believed that livestock suffered unnecessarily because people didn't understand their behavior well enough. She also thought no one gave much attention to the animals' well-being because people don't like to think about death.

Temple decided that her special abilities – at understanding cows and designing machines – gave her a special destiny. That destiny was to make the treatment of livestock kinder, or more humane. By reducing the stress on animals, she could give greater dignity to both their life and their death.

Temple had to work hard convincing people in the farm and meat industry that their operations could be improved by new designs – and that her experience with cows gave her the ability to design these improvements. For example, ranch workers who yelled at cows all day to keep them moving had trouble believing Temple when she told them that a cow will voluntarily enter a properly-designed chute. Eventually, however, the meat industry welcomed Temple's ideas for reducing stress on livestock, because stressed cows waste valuable time and money.

Every rancher had seen a spooked cow jump easily over the side walls of a chute, which are about five and a half feet high or the height of an average woman. Once scared, a cow can take hours to calm down enough to move willingly through the chute. In addition, stress causes the release of substances inside a cow's body, like adrenaline, which last over a period of 24 hours and affect the meat, which then sells for less. Temple won the farm and meat industry over to her cause because her humane chute designs kept cows calm. And that saved money.

Temple's Innovations

Temple believed that the same disabilities that prevented her from understanding people gave her an intimate sensitivity to cows. She figured out how to work with their natural behavior instead of using brute force or fear. If a cow balked in a chute, Temple didn't blame the cow. Instead, she examined why the chute had made the cow fearful.

Whenever the ranch hands thought cattle were misbehaving or rebelling, Temple could see that the cows were afraid. She understood cows because of the ways they were similar to her. She saw them shy away from eye contact. She learned about "prey animals" – grazing animals like cows that don't eat meat, in contrast with predators or scavengers. Prey animals are calm, but always on the lookout for danger, with senses as finely-tuned as hers. She became able to read cows, to determine their well-being by watching the whites of their eyes and the movement of their ears and of their whole bodies.

Temple figured out that the same things that made her

panic also upset cows – especially rapid movements and sharp contrasts, like a dark-colored surface against a light one. She saw that cattle notice unexpected details in their environment that most people miss – from a moving branch to a small piece of jiggling chain to anything out of place: a puddle of water, a piece of paper, shiny things, people up ahead. She watched cattle jump at the same sounds that startled her, not fingernails on blackboards but loud human noises. When Temple stayed in a hotel room, someone whistling on the street five floors below could make her heart pound.

Temple traced the cows' reactions to the behavior of prey animals in the wild. Rapid movement can signal a wolf in the bushes, high-pitched voices can be a fellow prey animal's distress call, and eye contact can mean a threat or a challenge.

Temple discovered that to keep the cows calm and prevent them from being hurt, upsetting sights and sounds needed to be eliminated. Because their eyes are on the sides of their heads, cattle have wide-angle vision. Therefore, the walls of the chutes should be solid to prevent cows from seeing any outside distractions. Pointing out that cows' ears are very sensitive, and noises make them panic, Temple instructed drivers and ranch workers to be quiet. Drivers used to shout at cattle to get them off the trucks and then yell louder if they didn't move.

Temple observed that livestock have a natural circling

tendency, as if they think they are circling back to a safe place where they came from, rather than heading off into the unknown. Curves, therefore, comfort cattle. And in curved chutes, cattle can't become frightened by what's at the other end, because they can't see that far. Instead, the cows watch the rear end of their buddies in front, and since herd animals like to stay together, they feel content.

To some people, these innovations may appear to play mean tricks on the cows. But Temple believed she was at the helm of an important crusade to save animals from unnecessary pain and suffering before their deaths, deaths that could not be avoided.

When Temple built her first ramp for the immense Swift plant in Arizona, she thought her design would lead cows to such a peaceful death that she named it after a popular song, *Stairway to Heaven*. During her lectures, Temple was asked repeatedly whether cows know when they're going to be killed. Her answer was that, if cows knew they were going to die, they'd look more agitated. She believed that cows proceeding along her ramps look the same as cows heading for an ordinary medical exam. Temple pointed out that cows are less scared of her ramps than they are of a white plastic bottle rolling around in the dirt – because of its irregular movement and the contrast of dark and light.

Another of Temple's innovations improved the dip vat, a 7-foot deep swimming pool full of chemicals that remove bugs like lice. Cows enter the dip vat by walking down a ramp, which Temple converted from steel to deeply-grooved concrete to prevent slipping. If she had a cow's body and hooves, she said, she would be afraid to step on a slick and slippery metal ramp and would much prefer the concrete.

The invention for which Temple received the most acclaim is called a "center-track restrainer system" which is used to reduce the stress when moving an animal. A cow or sheep walks through a narrow corridor that has a metal bar running down the center of its floor, like the single rail of a train track. The walking animal straddles the metal bar, with his legs on either side, like a person on a bicycle. Gradually, as the ramp under his feet begins to decline, the center track comes up against the cow's belly to support him and move him along. Before the cow knows it, his feet are off the ground and he's being carried along, resting on this wide track as if he's on a comfortable conveyor belt. A false floor prevents the animal from seeing, and then becoming upset, that he's no longer on the ground. Cows photographed riding on the restrainer look peaceful and happy.

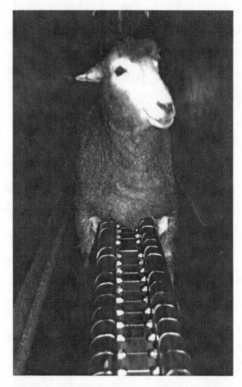

When Temple designed the center-track restrainer, she could tell how an animal would feel moving through her system.

***

When Temple was developing the restrainer, a plant operator named Mike Chabot offered to let her try it out on his cows. He said, "She was so totally committed to doing what she wanted to do, and she told me, 'I know this could work. I know we could do this better.' Temple and I have struck up a relationship that will last the rest of my life, I'm sure."

***

Temple's restrainer system was eventually adopted by every major brand meat producer – each of those for whom Temple had worked early in her career. It was the one invention for which she did obtain a patent and made some money, although, as she insisted, her goal was not to make money but "to make things better."

Getting Along with Others

Throughout her life, Temple never got better at understanding people. She compared herself to Mr. Spock on *Star Trek* – and later to the android, DATA – whose actions were determined by pure logic and not by emotion. She felt like a visitor to Earth from a faraway planet, who must watch the alien humans carefully in order to act like them. A well-known neurologist, Oliver Sacks, wrote a book about Temple entitled *An Anthropologist on Mars*, which is how Temple described herself, because she needed to study the humans around her as intensively as an anthropologist would study people in ancient or primitive cultures to understand their behavior.

In his book, Dr. Sacks described Temple as "a tall, strongly built woman in her mid-forties...wearing jeans, a knit shirt, western boots...I had the impression of a sturdy, no-nonsense cattlewoman, with an...absolute directness of manner and mind. She gave me a strong handshake and led the way down to her office."

Some of Temple's differences, like her obsessive attention, were advantageous. Temple concentrated completely on her work, whereas her co-workers became distracted by everything from competition with colleagues to where to buy new shoes. Temple paid little attention to clothes, cleanliness or hair-dos – like Albert Einstein with his wild, unstylish hair. She had no time for small talk or office chitchat. But sometimes her lack of concern for fellow workers got Temple into trouble.

***

Early in her designing career, Temple learned a hard lesson. When she saw a drawing by a colleague named George, Temple knew her design was much better.

"Yours won't work, George," she told him. But she didn't stop there. She didn't think about George's feelings.

"How can engineers be so stupid?" she asked him. She bent over his drawing to point out the sharp angles of the walkway that would scare the cows. "Can't you see where your design won't work? A corner like that makes a cow feel terrified of what it can't see. I know, because that's exactly how corners make me feel."

George stood up so abruptly he knocked his coffee cup off the desk and walked out of the office without a word. Temple remained with her feet glued to the floor as if she'd received an electrical shock. She couldn't leave the office.

When her boss, Jack, found her standing there, he said kindly, "You're right Temple. George knows it. He just told me."

"Whew," Temple said. "Because he was mad."

"That's right. You can't talk to people like that," Jack said. "You need to march up to the cafeteria and apologize to him publicly. Now. Also, if you're going to bend over people, use this." He handed her a pale blue jar labeled "Secret."

"What's that Jack?" Temple asked. "Do you have a secret for me?"

"Temple," Jack sighed. "It's a deodorant. You don't smell good. We're working on making you less weird."

***

Luckily, Temple's bosses considered her skills so valuable that they were often willing to help with her unusual behavior. As Temple said, "I am what I do, and that has worked for me." At a meeting where engineers ignored Temple because of her loud voice and wringing hands, she brought out one of her dip vat drawings. "You drew that?" they said, impressed. The strong respect that co-workers like Mike Chabot developed for Temple's work led to real friendships. Eventually Temple understood that faults in others' designs occurred not because they were stupid, but because they lacked her special ability to visualize.

Temple Grandin became the country's most expert designer of livestock facilities and was eventually responsible for over half of those used in the United States. She was proud of herself and the work of her company, Grandin Livestock Handling Systems, Inc., in improving the lives of these animals.

Temple Takes On McDonald's

For years, animal rights protesters had been demanding improvement in the treatment of animals. But not much happened in the industry until Temple developed a rating system. Her system determined the exact degree of kindness or cruelty to animals in each plant based on concrete measurements of the animals' levels of stress.

Temple studied thousands of cows, and the more she listened to them, the more she realized the key to their stress was their moos. Cows' moos tell how they feel. Temple's principal standard measured how many cows in each group going through a plant mooed or "vocalized."

If less than 3% of a herd – or 3 out of every 100 cows – made noise, that meant the herd was generally calm because the plant was treating them well.

Annie Farrell, an advisor to small farmers in New England who worked with Temple, called her "one cool cowboy." As Farrell described Temple's standards: "A cow must go from birth to death calm and quiet, without making a noise."

Before Temple, industry executives had become fed up with general accusations and complaints made by animal rights protesters because there was no clear course of action to follow. They were relieved when Temple provided standards with numerical measurements that they could understand and use. Temple's standards became the American Meat Industry Guidelines and were eventually adopted by other countries, led by Australia.

The McDonald's Corporation – producer of more hamburgers than any other fast-food company in the world – hired Temple to be Chief Consultant on Animal Welfare. She convinced McDonald's that, as the most powerful fast-food company in the world, it could force the entire industry to change.

The huge improvements made by McDonald's can be traced to public pressure, but the company also saved untold amounts of money with Temple's improvements. McDonald's executives said the company could have done nothing without Temple. Her first job was to train auditors to inspect the plants used by McDonald's. Suppliers who failed the stress inspections were fired. Soon other fast food chains like Burger King and Wendy's also hired Temple to impose her standards.

Temple's Life

Temple Grandin has never married, but as an adult she became closer to her brother and one sister when she realized how much they had in common with her as either visual thinkers or animal lovers. She has also made friends through shared interests like animal behavior or autism. But, like cows, Temple became most attached to places, and often went out of her way to revisit ranches and buildings where she had worked.

Temple became a popular lecturer around the U.S. on the two subjects of her expertise: humane designs for livestock and autism. She complained that she traveled so much, she saw more airplanes than cows. When she'd finished work at a plant – whether creating new designs or inspecting the cows' well-being – Temple would return to her apartment in the Rocky Mountains. She'd head straight for her squeeze machine, which gave her comforting squeezes and better dreams.

In a famous documentary film called *Stairway to Heaven*, Temple Grandin looks happiest during the long, silent scenes when she is alone with cows. She walks slowly around their huge pen and sits among the cows until they stop backing away. Slowly they begin to push up against her – as if she were one of them, a cow.

Printed in the United States
62925LVS00002B/1-3